Volume Eight
Later Intermediate

Accent on GILLOCK

by William Gillock

CONTENTS

ISBN 978-0-87718-083-8

EXCLUSIVELY DISTRIBUTED BY

HAL•LEONARD®

Visit Hal Leonard Online at
www.halleonard.com

Contact us:
Hal Leonard
7777 West Bluemound Road
Milwaukee, WI 53213
Email: info@halleonard.com

In Europe, contact:
Hal Leonard Europe Limited
42 Wigmore Street
Marylebone, London, W1U 2RN
Email: info@halleonardeurope.com

In Australia, contact:
Hal Leonard Australia Pty. Ltd.
4 Lentara Court
Cheltenham, Victoria, 3192 Australia
Email: info@halleonard.com.au

To Yvonne Reynolds

Arabesque Sentimentale

William Gillock

22
L.H.
R.H.
27
L.H.
R.H.
L.H.
R.H.
31
L.H.
dim.
R.H.
R.H.
rit.
mp a tempo
35
cresc. poco a poco
40
f
rit.
p a tempo
mp
45
mf
f
R.H.
p
L.H.
L.H.
mf
pp
8vb

For the 25th Anniversary of the Joplin, Missouri Piano Teachers Association

Night Serenade

William Gillock

20
3
24
3
mf
tre corde
28
2
1
2
32
a tempo
36
p
40
cresc.
1
4
1
1
2
3
8va
rit.
f
mp
p

Portrait of Paris

William Gillock

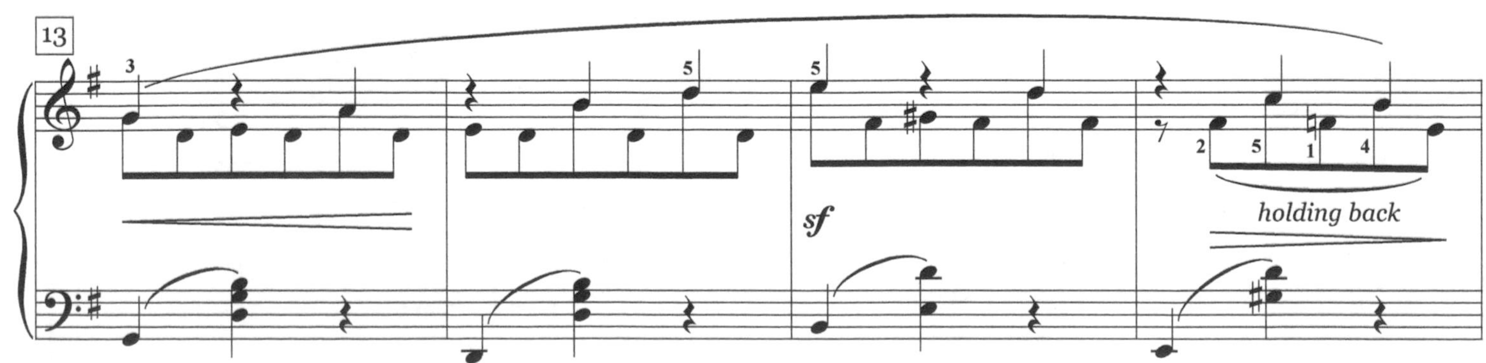

17
mf a tempo
21
26
increasing little by little
31
holding back
ff
sf
sf
sf
sf
sf
sf
35
mf a tempo
simile

39
sf

43

47
sf
holding back

8va
51
f a tempo

56
61
66
holding back
Cadenza-like (begin slowly, accelerate)
Slowly

Sleighbells in the Snow

William Gillock

9
(8va)
f
pp
11
p
13
mf
15
f
cresc.
17
sf
pp
sf

19
L.H.
p
22
mf
f
cresc.
25
ff
28
sfz
mf
30
mp

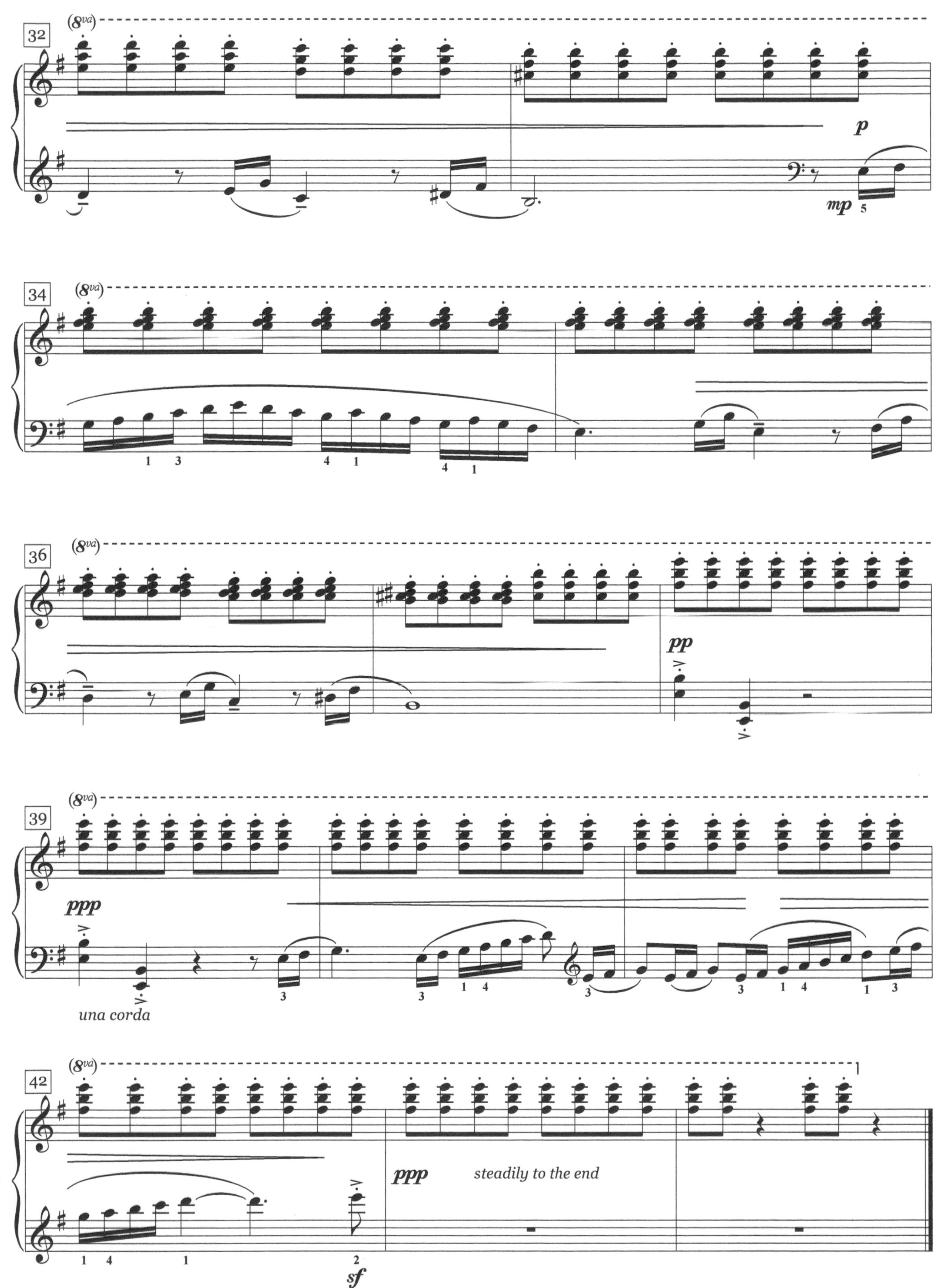

32
(8va)
p
mp
34
(8va)
36
(8va)
pp
39
(8va)
ppp
una corda
42
(8va)
ppp
steadily to the end
sf

To the New Jersey Music Education Council, Inc.

Goldfish

William Gillock

In a flowing manner, but with much flexibility

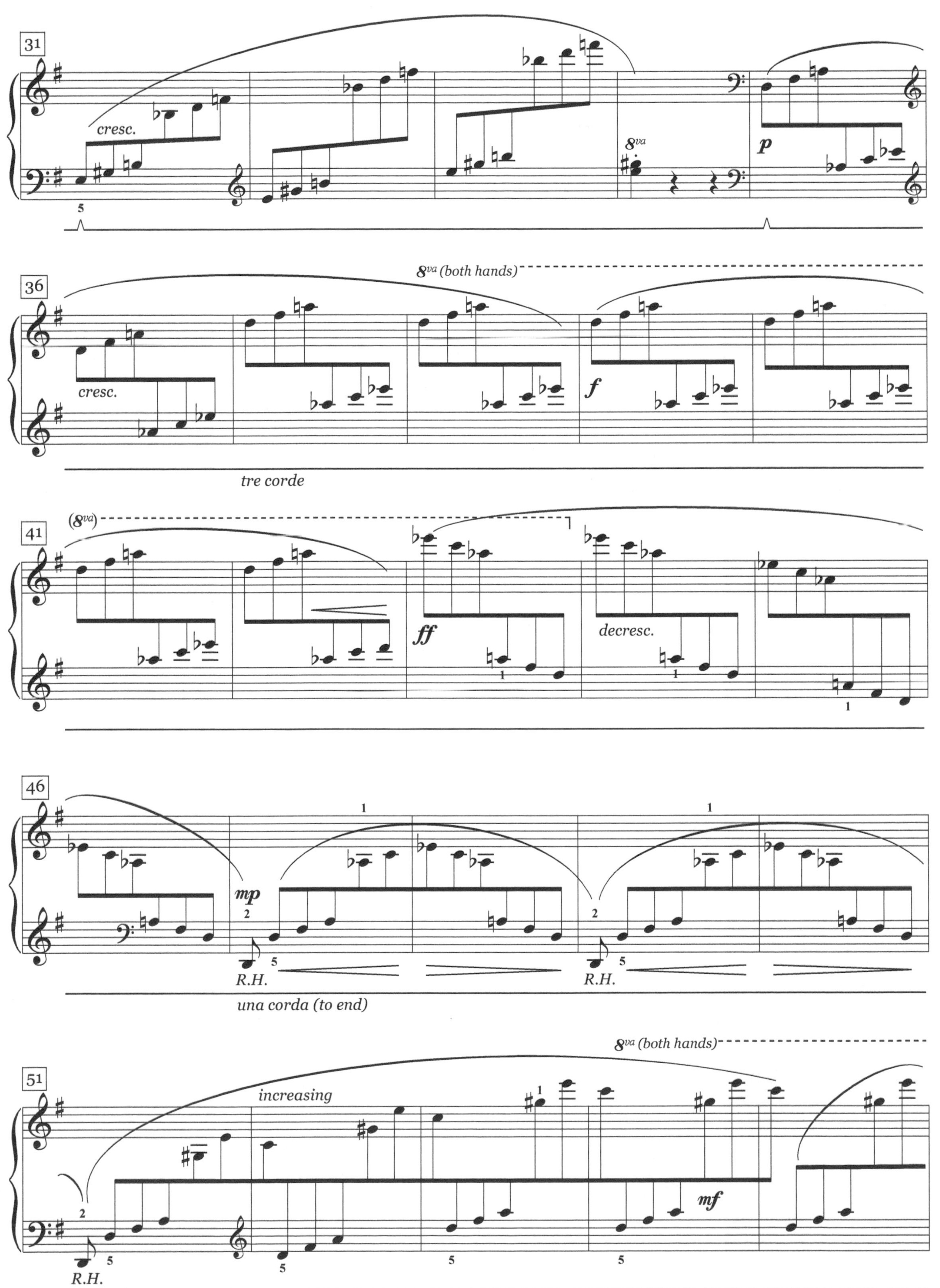

31
cresc.
8va
p
36
8va (both hands)
cresc.
f
tre corde
41
(8va)
ff
decresc.
46
mp
R.H.
una corda (to end)
R.H.
51
8va (both hands)
increasing
mf
R.H.

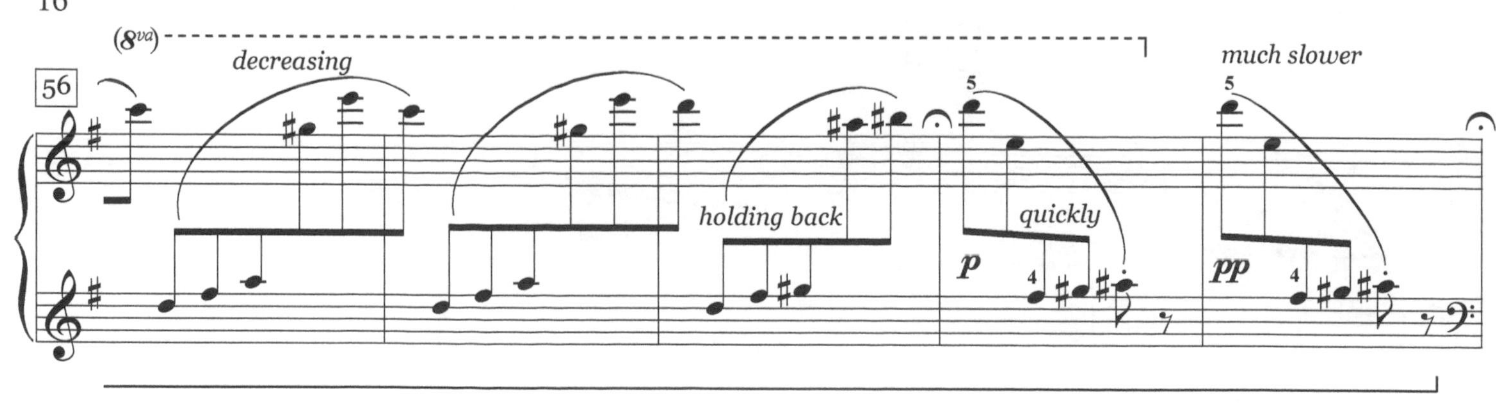
(8va)
decreasing
56
5
5
much slower
holding back
quickly
p
4
pp
4

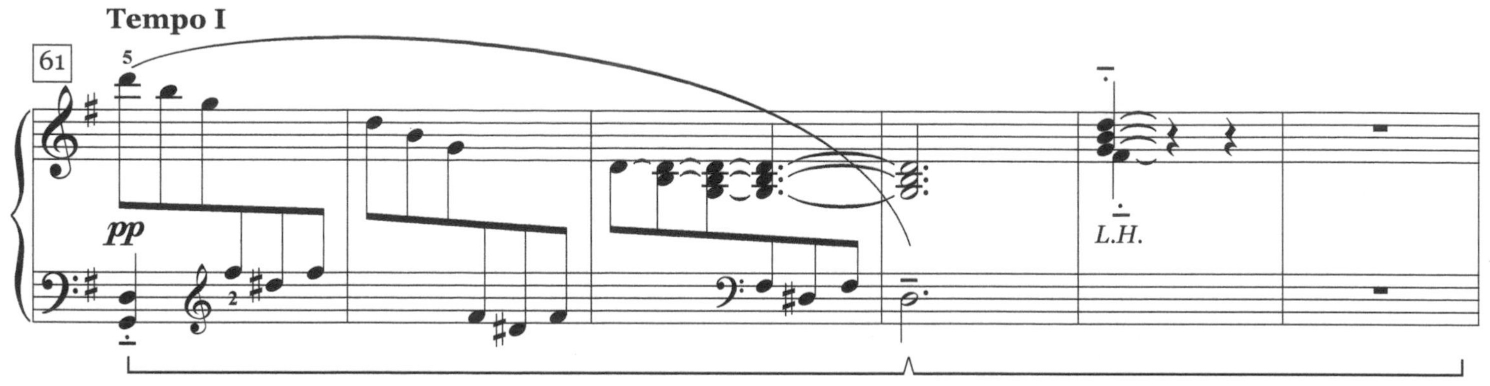
Tempo I
61
5
pp
2
L.H.

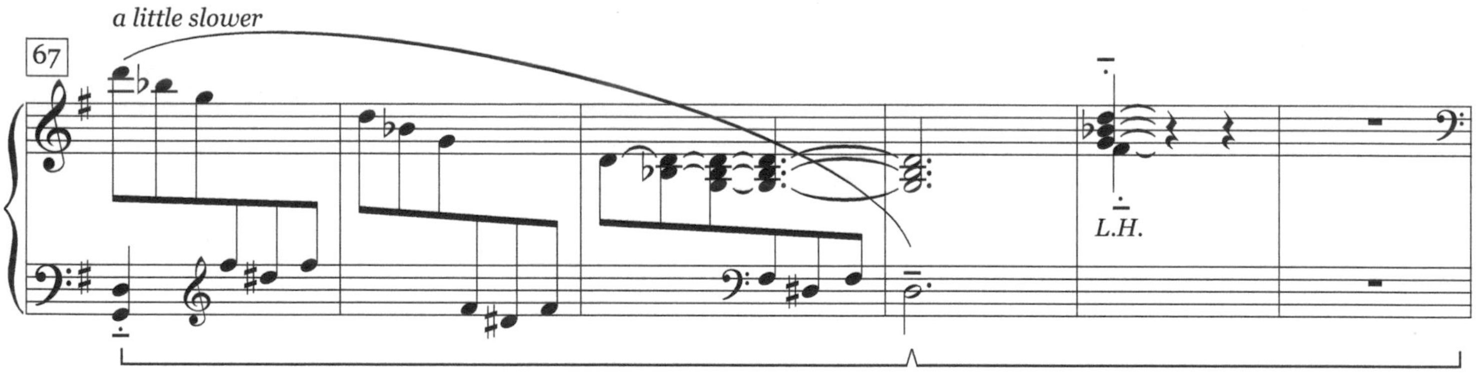
a little slower
67
L.H.

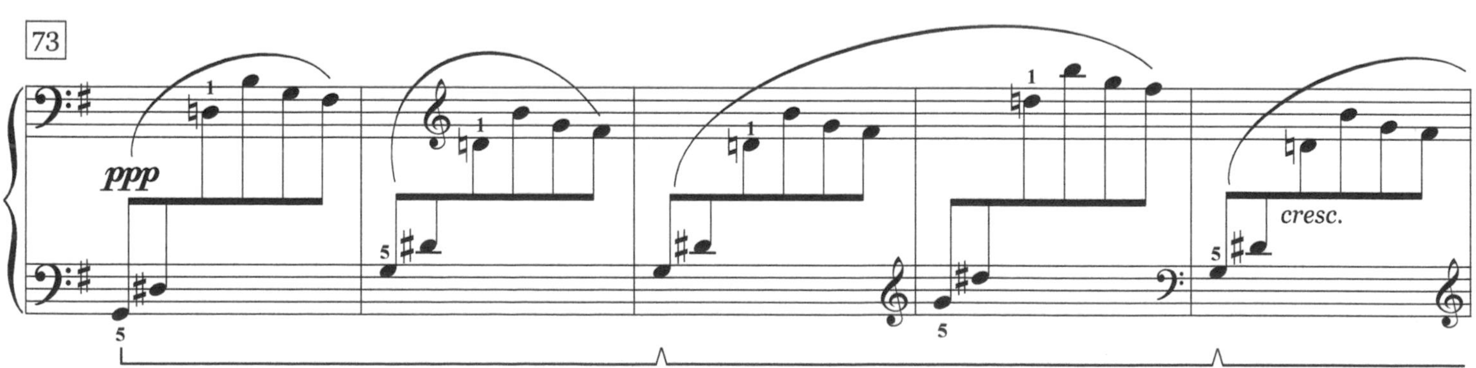
73
ppp
1
1
1
1
5
5
cresc.
5
5

78
decresc.
rit.
ppp